Tracing Our ITALIAN Roots

KATHLEEN LEE

John Muir Publications
Santa Fe, New Mexico

Special thanks to Louise Pioli, Miriam Sagan, Gerald Lee, and Terry Passalacqua.

This book is dedicated to Robert Pioli.

John Muir Publications, P.O. Box 613, Santa Fe, New Mexico 87504
© 1993 by John Muir Publications
All rights reserved. Published 1993

Printed in the United States of America

First edition. First printing September 1993
          First TWG printing September 1993

Library of Congress Cataloging-in-Publication Data
Lee, Kathleen.
American origins : tracing our Italian roots / by Kathleen Lee
      p.   cm.
      Includes index.
Summary: Depicts the wave of Italian immigration to America at the beginning of
the twentieth century, describing the life left behind in Italy and the challenges
faced in America. Includes brief discussions of some prominent Italian Americans.
ISBN 1-56261-149-6 : $12.95
1. Italian Americans—History—Juvenile literature. [1. Italian
Americans—History.] I. Title.
E184.I8L44 1993
973'.0451—dc20   93-5149
                                                                   CIP
                                                                   AC

Logo Design: Peter Aschwanden
Interior Design: Ken Wilson
Illustrations: Beth Evans and Nate Butler
Typography: Ken Wilson
Printer: Arcata Graphics/Kingsport

Distributed to the book trade by
W. W. Norton & Co., Inc.
500 Fifth Ave.
New York, New York 10110

Distributed to the education
market by
The Wright Group
19201 120th Avenue N.E.
Bothell, WA 98011-9512

Cover photo, The Bettmann Archive
Back cover photo, Library of Congress

CONTENTS

The Bettmann Archive

INTRODUCTION

Cristoforo Colombo sailed for the King and Queen of Spain, but he was an Italian—the very first Italian ever to set eyes on the land so many Italians would later call home. Other Italian explorers also navigated the coasts of America. Amerigo Vespucci, from Florence, told people that the continent was not part of Asia, as they believed, but was a New World. America is in fact named for this explorer. And Giovanni da Verrazzano, from Tuscany, was probably the first European to sail into New York Bay, in 1524.

Italy is not a large country. It's long and narrow and shaped like a boot. Each part of Italy is different. The North gave birth to the great art and science of the Italian Renaissance in the 1600s and, later, to the movement to unify Italy as one country in 1871. Central Italy is the home of the headquarters of the Catholic Church, Vatican City, where the Pope resides. The South, poorer than the North, has beautiful land; the people who live there are mostly farmers. For hundreds of years, foreigners conquered the South to use the land for their own benefit.

Up until 1860 most of the Italians who came to America as immigrants were from northern Italy. They were curious adventurers, or Protestants leaving a Catholic country, or glassblowers invited to lend their skills to building the new country. The voyage across

How Many Italians Came to America?

Decade	Number
1820-1830	439
1831-1840	2,253
1841-1850	1,870
1851-1860	9,231
1861-1870	11,725
1871-1880	55,759
1881-1890	307,309
1891-1900	651,893
1901-1910	2,045,877
1911-1920	1,109,524
1921-1930	455,315
1931-1940	68,028
1941-1950	57,661

Nate Butler

The voyage from Italy to America was long and dangerous

An immigrant family gazes at New York City from the dock of Ellis Island

the ocean in the early days was very long and dangerous.

The large numbers of Italians who immigrated to America at the end of the 1800s were from southern Italy. Boatload after boatload left Naples, the main southern Italian port city. So many people poured out of southern Italy, it's hard to believe anyone was left behind! From 1901 to 1910, more than 2 million Italians left Italy for America—which meant that more than 500 Italians arrived in America *every day* for ten years.

After 1920 the number of people leaving Italy decreased. In 1924 the U.S. government passed a law allowing only a certain number of people from each country to immigrate to America. Only 3,845 Italians could enter the United States each year. Americans were reluctant to admit many more foreigners into the country and didn't believe that Italians could be true Americans. Italians who were already here had the difficult task of convincing other Americans that they could be as loyal as any citizen in the country.

Italians came to America hoping for a better life than they had had in Italy. They expected to find the pot of gold at the end of the rainbow when they stepped off the boat onto the shores of New York City. Of course, the good life didn't come so easily. They had to fight against prejudice and survive hard living conditions. They had to struggle to be accepted as Americans. Even so, America offered more work and opportunity than Italy could. Because of the Italian Americans' hard work and ingenuity, their dream of a better life eventually came true and they contributed much to America.

FAMILY LIFE

Our story focuses on the Italian farmers of southern Italy, who made up the majority of Italian immigrants. Imagine you are part of such a family, one hundred years ago. Your small town is filled with your cousins, second cousins, even third cousins, and you know them all. If your mother gets sick, aunts and grandmothers come over to cook or work in the garden. Everybody in the family helps and watches out for each other— which means your behavior has to be perfect! If somebody catches you bothering a neighbor's donkey, for example, you are in big trouble. You are not allowed to embarrass your family or bring shame to them. Your friends call you by the family nickname, perhaps "big pasta" or "fat peacock."

At the center of your family is your mother. She feeds the family with the little food there is, takes care of you when you get sick, and makes sure you work hard and behave yourself. She is friendly with the neighbors and the mill owner, so he gives her a good deal on flour. Your father is the bread-winner of the family. He is in charge of finding work for everyone in the family and taking care of any problems with town officials.

Your only toys are a few handcarved wooden horses. At school, your teachers are priests. They are strict and rap your knuckles with a stick when you misbehave. By the time you are 12 years old, childhood is over. You stop going to school because the family needs the money you can make working to help pay for food, taxes, and rent. Everyone in the

In Italy it is sometimes said that there are two countries in one. Just as in the United States there are regional differences in accents, food, and lifestyles, so there are differences in Italy. Many people in the North think the South is uneducated, full of small-town attitudes and superstitions. Many people in the South think the North is unfriendly, snobbish, and lacking in common sense. In cuisine, the North is known for light creamy pasta sauces, the South for its tangy tomato sauces. At one time, the dialects were so different that people from the North and the South could not understand each other.

Beth Evans

The regions of Italy

Young Italians enjoy a spaghetti lunch at an outdoor restaurant in Naples

family helps out. Your sisters work at home washing clothes, cleaning, and taking care of the animals. Your brothers work in the fields or with your father.

Food is simple and not always abundant in the *Mezzogiorno*, as southern Italy is called in Italian. Breakfast and lunch consist of figs, tomatoes, and homemade bread. The entire family eats supper together—bread, fresh pasta with olive oil, tomato sauce or eggplant, or a bean soup. Mama passes out forks and spoons, and everyone eats from a single large bowl. Only rarely is there sausage, wine, cheese, or fish. Olives, citrus fruits, and grapes are plentiful during successful crop years.

Your family lives in a one-room house, with the chickens sleeping beneath the big bed and the donkey braying beside the pig in the corner. When it is available, water is collected from the well in the *piazza*, the town courtyard. Light comes from candles. You love the clean air, the mountains around your town, your donkey, and the flowers in the

spring. You like teasing your cousins after the supper chores are finished, and you play in the nearby creek amid the pollywogs and frogs.

Hanging homemade noodles out to dry

COMMUNITY, WORK, AND RELIGION

Your southern Italian town perches on top of a hill. Long ago, people moved to the hilltops so they could spot trouble coming from bandits or invaders. After the invasions ended, the villagers remained on the hilltops, enjoying the cool breezes and beautiful views.

The houses in the village are made of mud and stone, which look golden in the setting sun. The streets are narrow cobblestone passageways, just wide enough for a donkey loaded with kindling to pass through. The center of life in the town is the piazza, the courtyard where the well and the church are. The sound of the church bell, *il campanile*, marks the boundary of your world. Nobody in your family travels farther than the sound of *il campanile*. Priests live in a monastery at the edge of town.

People entertain themselves by talking with their neighbors and playing musical instruments. They sit in the narrow streets exchanging news; the women mend or sew, and the men smoke or play cards. The women stand in line at the well with their copper pots on their hips, chatting while they wait for their turn. On hot evenings, they walk around the piazza to cool off. You and the other children chase chickens and each other, trying to turn your chores into games. Winter feels endless. It's too cold to play outdoors and you argue with your brothers and sisters. Summers are wonderful but very hot, with dry, blistering winds.

Your father rents fields from a man

Italians prayed at shrines in their homes

Your mother teaches you that religion isn't just about going to church on Sundays. She talks to God, the saints, and the Holy Family as if they were special friends. She tells them about your sister's illness, the drought, or an earthquake. Trouble is *mal occhio*—the "evil eye"—and Mother is always trying to keep it away from her family. You wear a good luck bag around your neck that contains a garlic clove and small replicas of animal horns. There is a shrine to the Madonna in your house, and you pray to Santa Bologna for healthy teeth, San Antonio to safeguard your animals, and Santa Barbara to protect you from lightning. Each saint is honored with a special day of celebration.

Dramatic cliffs and a shady grape arbor in the beautiful coastal town of Amalfi

who lives in Naples. One of your uncles doesn't even have a piece of land to rent, and he is always looking for work building roads or laboring in the fields. Another uncle owns a small piece of land, but it isn't large enough to support his family, so he too is always looking for work. The men walk before dawn to the fields with their tools and their donkeys, work all day, and return wearily as the sun sets. There are no tractors or fertilizers; they till the land with hand plows, hoes, and shovels.

And there is never enough work. Often, the men lean against the stone walls of the piazza, talking, worrying, and hoping. If they have crops planted, they worry about drought and disease. If they are out of work, they worry about paying rent and taxes.

There are also shopkeepers, shoemakers, bakers, and blacksmiths in the village, but even they work in the fields to make enough money to survive. If the farmers have a bad year, so does everyone else in town. Everyone is dependent on each other.

Boys picking lemons in Palermo, Sicily

POLITICS AND CRIME

In the Old Country, you were taught that your family was more important than anything. Italy was a country of thousands of families, each wanting the government to do what was best for their family, even if it might not be best for others.

Southern Italy was poorer than northern Italy. The government favored the North with more roads and better schools. Northerners had more choices for work. They could work in factories or construction, farming or food production.

In the South, families still grew their own food, made their own clothing, and struggled to survive off the land as they always had. There were few roads, no factories, and no farm machines. Time seemed to stand still. Only a few farmers owned land.

Most worked for rich landowners who lived in the cities. If a man didn't own land, he couldn't vote.

As the population continued to grow, there was even less food and work to go around. Your parents had dreams: they wanted to buy shoes for their children, live in a two-room house, and own land. But these things seemed impossible, and the government could not be relied on for help.

These desperate conditions led to the growth of crime. In southern Italy, people were so poor that some stole to escape the difficulty of finding work and providing food for their families. You were taught as a child that you could trust the people in your family and your town, but no one else. So, oddly, stealing from your townspeople didn't really seem like stealing. It felt more like taking what you needed from people in your own family.

Villagers spot a man coming to poison their cow

Townspeople often distrusted the priests, who usually took sides with the wealthy landowners against the peasants. In one town, all of the cows were mysteriously dying one by one. Two men sat up all night in their pasture, watching their cows and waiting to see what would happen. At dawn, they caught a man coming to poison the animals. The local priest had hired him to kill the cows in secret, hoping the townspeople would think it was God's will. The priest wanted the people to remain poor so they would have to work for the wealthy landowners.

Poor living and working conditions in the villages sometimes led to crime. Here, farmers thresh wheat by hand.

In some cases crime became a way of life and even an accepted part of the community. A common scheme was called selling "protection." A criminal would tell the local fisherman, for example, that he had to pay the criminal to protect the fisherman from thieves and vandals. If the fisherman refused, the criminal and his partners would beat up the fisherman or damage his boat or his house. Eventually, the fisherman would agree to pay the criminal money or give him a percentage of his daily catch.

Seldom did the villages have police forces to protect the people. Usually, one powerful criminal would gain control over a village. He would not allow other thieves to live in the village. In this way he truly did protect the villagers. Often, if a villager needed to borrow money he would go to the criminal to ask for help. The criminal would loan him the money, but at a very high interest rate. In this way, the criminal, and the people who worked for him, became both respected and feared by the village people.

A fisherman is persuaded to buy "protection"

FAMOUS ITALIANS OF THE OLD COUNTRY

Marco Polo (1254–1324)

Marco Polo was one of the most remarkable travelers the world has ever known. He was born in Venice while his father was away traveling in China. He didn't meet his father until he returned when Marco was 15 years old. Two years later, Marco left for China with his father, Niccolo, and his uncle Maffeo. They crossed the fierce deserts of Central Asia and traveled into eastern China. For the next 17 years, Marco traveled through the deserts and jungles of Asia, where no European had ever been before. When the Polos finally returned home in 1295, their family was shocked to see them. They had long thought they were all dead. Marco was thrown in jail a year later by the Genoese (natives of Genoa), who were at war with the Venetians (natives of Venice). In prison he shared a cell with a writer, and Marco began to dictate the story of his journey. The stories were published as *Il Milione* (*The Million*) and are called *The Travels of Marco Polo* in English. This book has become a classic, though in Marco's day few Italians believed it was true. On his deathbed Marco was asked to admit that the book was all lies. Instead, he said that he hadn't told even half of what he had seen.

Michelangelo (1475–1564)

When Michelangelo was a child in school, he liked drawing better than studying. While the teacher lectured about mathematics and sci-

A drawing from Polo's book about his travels

Daniel de Votterra's portrait of Michelangelo

Michelangelo's La Pietà

Michelangelo was probably Renaissance Italy's most brilliant artist. Some of his famous works include *La Pietà, David, Moses,* and the *Bruges Madonna.*

Giovanni Boccaccio (1313–1375)

Boccaccio was a famous Italian storyteller. Born in Paris, he lived most of his life in Naples and Rome. His father wanted him to go into business or law. But at age 15 he quit his law studies to write stories. It took him ten years to finish his most famous work, the *Decameron*, a collection of 100 tales. In this book ten people, seven women and three men, flee the Black Death in Florence in 1348. The Black Death was what people called the plague that swept through Europe in Boccaccio's time, killing one quarter of the population. This disease, now known as bubonic plague, was an infectious fever caused by rat fleas; it spread quickly in the crowded cities. In the *Decameron*, the ten people tell each other stories over a period of ten days. Even though the book portrays the terrible plague, the tales are funny and clever. They show the mistakes and embarrassments common to all human beings.

ence, young Michelangelo sketched a detailed, exact drawing of his own hand. Michelangelo was sent to school in Florence, where he lived with a stonemason's family. His father was unhappy when Michelangelo accepted an apprenticeship with a famous painter, Domenico Ghirlandaio; he didn't want his son to be an artist. Soon Michelangelo's talent was noticed by the Medici family, one of the great families of the Renaissance. Michelangelo became a master of painting and sculpting the human body. His sculptures are so lifelike you almost expect them to walk towards you or lift their heads and speak. One of his most famous paintings covers the ceiling of the Sistine Chapel in Rome. He painted it lying on his back on a scaffold, and it took him four years to complete!

The famous Italian storyteller Giovanni Boccaccio as a young man

FAMOUS ITALIANS OF THE OLD COUNTRY

Maria Montessori (1870–1952)

Maria Montessori was the first woman in Italy to become a doctor, in 1894. Her greatest interest was to help children. First, she opened a school in Rome for mentally impaired children. Her goal was to design a school where children could be creative and express themselves without any restrictions. She began with a school for children aged three to six and later opened a school for older children. Now there are Montessori schools all over the world, teaching children of all levels, following the ideas of this extraordinary Italian woman.

Marconi (right) tests an early radio transmitter

Guglielmo Marconi (1874–1937)

Have you ever seen an old Western movie in which a couple of men at the railroad station tap out an urgent message in Morse code on a telegraph machine? Well, before 1895, telegraphic messages were sent along a wire. Later, thanks to the experiments of Guglielmo Marconi in northern Italy, signals could be sent without a wire. Marconi was an inventor and a physicist. He was fascinated with the complex science of electromagnetic waves, and he experimented with them until he discovered a way to send messages along these waves rather than along a wire. With wireless telegraphy, messages could easily be sent across great distances—even across oceans. Marconi was a pioneer in the technologies that have brought us such advanced systems as satellite transmissions. He won the Nobel Prize in physics in 1909.

Maria Montessori, doctor and teacher

Enzo Ferrari in a Sly Linder racing car, 1924

Ettore Bugatti (1882–1947) and Enzo Ferrari (1898–1988)

Italy makes some fabulously fast cars: the Alfa Romeo, Maserati, Bugatti, and Ferrari. Ettore Bugatti might be considered the father of Italian racing cars. He began designing fast cars in 1899, and his models won races throughout the 1930s. The Golden Bugatti was probably one of the most carefully built cars the world has ever seen. It was also one of the most expensive, and only six or eight models were ever made. Unfortunately, the company died when Bugatti did, as there was no one of equal talent to continue his work.

Enzo Ferrari began his life with cars as a race car driver for Alfa Romeo. Then he began designing his own cars. Ferrari cars have won nearly one quarter of all Grand Prix races. Ferraris are among the fastest and most famous cars ever made.

Some of the world's fastest cars were designed by Italians

DEBT AND DESPAIR

For most Italians in the southern region of the country, the struggle to survive became harder, not easier. The sighs of your mother and the grumblings of your father grew greater every year. Your father complained about the man who, living comfortably in Naples, cared nothing for the land he owned or for the man who worked on it. Your mother worried about her children's future.

After Italy became a single country in 1871, the peasants had to pay four different taxes: a national tax, a province tax, a local tax, and a family tax. The family tax taxed peasants for everything they owned—the burro they used in the fields, their chickens, their pig. People had never needed money before; they simply traded their crops or their labor to pay rent or to have their wheat ground into flour at the mill. But for taxes they needed money, which they did not have. Their debts grew and grew.

There were other pressures as well. By the end of the 19th century transportation had improved in Italy, so wheat and citrus

Southern Italians began to dream of America. In America, they said, anyone could rise to the top. You could start off digging ditches and end up a millionaire. You could begin as a garbage collector and one day become a respected and successful businessman. America was a country of equal opportunity where it didn't matter if you were poor, from Southern Italy, and couldn't read or write. Everyone was given a chance. America was a place of great beauty where everyone was treated with fairness. Italian emigrants had no idea what America was really like or what they would find when they arrived.

Italians had high hopes about America

A dilapidated apartment building in Naples

fruits could be moved without spoiling. Products from America began flowing into markets in France, Germany, and Switzerland, causing prices to drop. Italian produce came to be worth less than foreign produce. Then a disagreement between the Italians and the French flared up over taxes on imported wines. The French stopped buying Italian wines, almost ruining the Italian grape and wine industries.

Your father still worked his small farm with his shovel, hand plow, hoe, and donkey. He just couldn't keep up with the farmers outside southern Italy who could grow more with less effort. Because other farmers had machinery and fertilizers, they grew better crops faster and could charge less for their produce. Though your father worked harder, he actually made less money.

And the population of southern Italy kept growing. There were more mouths to feed and less land to support the growing number of people. Your uncle, who owned land, divided it among his children so each had a small piece. Then it was divided again among their children until several people had to share a single orange tree! For blacksmiths, tailors, stonemasons, and fishermen, life was hard because few townspeople could afford their services.

In Sicily, an island off the southern tip of Italy, people tried to improve their lives. They had meetings, talking late into the night by candlelight. Then they marched through town, demanding lower rents and higher wages. Policemen came and sent the farmers home. They weren't allowed to have meetings. Everything stayed the same. The Italian farmers realized there was no way to improve their lives, except to leave.

15

DISEASE AND NATURAL DISASTER

Every day you were hungry. In winter there wasn't enough wood to heat your house, and you didn't have a warm coat. Most of the trees in southern Italy and Sicily had been chopped down by foreign invaders and rulers. Without trees, the rich topsoil washed away, leaving behind dry, dusty earth that couldn't hold water or grow plants. Rocks poked through the thin soil of the stripped, bony mountains. The land looked sick and tired.

When it rained, the earth slid away because it was not anchored by the roots of trees and shrubs. Tremendous landslides and mudslides brought houses down with them. Villages barely clung to the edge of cliffs while the earth fell away below. Mud and rocks collected in ravines and valleys, blocking their entrances and making stagnant ponds. These ponds, in the warmth of summer, were perfect nesting spots for mosquitoes. Your grandmother and your aunt got malaria from the mosquitoes. Then in 1897 there was a

Mt. Vesuvius spews a plume of smoke

cholera epidemic and your sister and several cousins died. Illness and death added to the misery and defeat felt by everyone in the town.

There were also earthquakes and major volcanic eruptions of Mt. Vesuvius in southern Italy and Mt. Etna in Sicily. Mt. Vesuvius erupted six times between 1839 and 1872. After the 1852 eruption of Mt. Etna, which took many lives, there were regular eruptions through 1900. Entire villages were swallowed

With too much time on their hands, some Italian youngsters got into trouble

Roberto Pioli missed his father. His father had been in America for five years and his mother, Emma, had her hands full with four active children. Roberto was 11 years old and supposed to be working with a shoemaker. But there was never much work, so he ran around town or in the hills, looking for food. He would pick oranges off trees, or steal a bucket of milk or a chunk of cheese. Like the gangs we have in cities today, Roberto sometimes didn't know what to do with himself, and so he made trouble. Finally, Emma had had enough. She decided it was time to take all her children to America to be with their father.

Earthquakes, such as the one that hit Sicily in 1906, left many people homeless

by flowing lava, crops were buried, and animals and people died.

People wanted to escape, but they hesitated—at least these difficulties were familiar. A southern Italian proverb expresses the peasants' thinking: "He who leaves the old way for the new knows what he leaves but not what he will find." Would you give up everything to go to a strange place?

The first to emigrate from your town were single men. Their idea was to make quick money and return. Then fathers left for America, leaving behind wives and children. They too planned to return once they had enough money to buy land.

For many years, there were nearly as many Italians returning from America as there were going to it. These people were called "birds of passage," and they formed a regular tide going back and forth between Italy and America. But some men stayed in America and their brothers followed, to be joined later by wives and children. Slowly, Italians settled permanently in America, hoping for a better life and willing to work hard for it.

Papa sorrowfully boards his ship to America

17

CROSSING THE WIDE ATLANTIC

The voyage to America took up to twenty days, crossing 4,000 miles of ocean. It was a frightening journey for people who had never even gone ten miles outside their village. The opening of the port in Naples to immigrant ships and the development of faster, sturdier steel ships made the immigration of thousands of Italians possible. Then, in 1885, the United States government passed a law to protect immigrants from signing contracts to work in America in exchange for the price of their passage on the ship. These contracts further forced immigrants to turn over a portion of their paychecks for years to the contractor. Under the new law, immigrants were supposed to come without jobs already arranged, but with some money of their own. This was not an easy

Immigrants crowded together on deck

Emma Pioli and her four children endured three weeks of nearly constant seasickness. Darro, the youngest, was still recovering from the measles. Ebe, the oldest, had not wanted to leave; she missed her boyfriend back home and had little interest in America. She complained about the food, the smells, and the filth. Roberto spent all of his time in the galleys watching the cooks prepare the terrible food. The cooks teased him, pinched his cheeks, and gave him extra slices of bread. He snuck onto the second- and first-class decks to look into the private cabins, which were shared by only four or even two people! Domenico found some boys to play cards with hour after hour. At night, the whole family squeezed into two bunks and tried to sleep as people coughed, groaned, or argued late into the night. It seemed that the journey would never end.

Music and laughter break up the long days at sea

The Bettmann Archive

requirement. They were leaving because they had no money!

Most immigrants could only afford to travel steerage class. This meant that they traveled in the dark holds of the ship in crowded, unsanitary conditions. The ventilation was terrible and the food was so bad that most people could not eat it without becoming ill. The journey was long and grueling. People slept in their clothes beside their luggage. They lay in their bunks or on the hard floor day after day breathing the foul air. Sometimes they had to share their quarters with livestock and were kept awake by horses stomping all night. Or it was so crowded they could only occupy the bunks in shifts; one group waited on deck while the other group slept. To make matters worse, the ship crew bullied and shouted at the immigrants.

For the children it was a strange, exciting adventure, if sometimes exhausting. They had never been on a ship, seen so much water, or been among so many strangers. The adults were filled with anxiety about their arrival in America. What would they find?

Where would they live? They counted their few coins to make sure they still had them; they guarded against theft on the ship. They thought of the answers they would give to the men who would question them at the immigration office. What if the father or brother wasn't there to meet them? If they weren't expecting anyone to meet them, they worried about what they would do and where they would go.

The port of Naples

Library of Congress

THE ARRIVAL IN AMERICA

At the peak of immigration, between 1900 and 1920, 97 percent of Italian immigrants landed in New York. Ellis Island—called "Island of Tears" by Italians because their arrival was such an emotional experience—was the most famous processing center for immigrants.

The immigrants' arrival into America was frightening. So much happened that they did not understand. They waited in long lines in cavernous rooms with entire shiploads of immigrants, exhausted after their grueling voyage and still recovering from seasickness, terrible food, and bad air. Mounds of luggage were everywhere, children cried, and mothers frantically tried to keep everyone together.

The first line was for the medical inspection. At that time, doctors were especially concerned about eye diseases. Your head and body were examined, and then your eyes were carefully looked into, the eyelids pulled back for close inspection. If there was anything questionable, the doctor chalked a mark on your shoulder and led you aside for a special medical exam.

If you didn't pass the medical exam, you were sent back to Italy. If you passed the medical exam, you moved into the line for customs. There, officials asked you questions: How old are you? Who is waiting for you? Can you read? What is your job skill? How

The average amount of money in an immigrant's pocket on arrival was only $10. Immigrants were unaware of the dangers of a big city. Many had their money swindled or stolen within their first few hours in America. Perhaps a cab driver would demand ten times as much money for fare, or a shopkeeper would charge twice as much for an apple and then give incorrect change. By the end of the first day, the greenhorn (as the new immigrants were called) knew that the reality of America would be very different from the dream.

The Bettmann Archive

A health officer examines young immigrants

Italian men and boys wait to go through customs at Ellis Island

much money do you have? If you were well-prepared, you would have a few borrowed coins to show the inspector that you had money. This question made no sense to you because you had come to America to *make* money! Any hesitation in responding to these questions, or any conflicting answers, made the inspector suspicious. Then he might bully you or send you to the Special Inquiry line, where officials would examine your case closely and decide your fate in a courtroom-like setting. If your answers didn't satisfy the inspector, you would be sent back to Italy.

After clearing customs you ascended "The Stairs of Separation." It was here that individuals and sometimes even families parted ways, perhaps not to see one another for a long time. Those who were going on to other cities such as Chicago or St. Louis followed the hallways to "Railroads," which led to the ferry going to the train station. Immigrants known as "New York Outsides" went down the stairs to take the ferry to New York City, to

begin their life in America. "New York Detained" went to rooms to await the relatives or friends who were meeting them. Sometimes people waited for days for their fathers or sponsors, sleeping in the barracks and eating food as bad as it was on the ship. If no one arrived after a couple of weeks and they had nowhere to go, they were sent back to Italy.

Waiting in line for the ferry to New York City

LEARNING THE LANGUAGE

America needed unskilled workers to build subways, roads, railroads, and buildings. It needed people to work in its factories. The Italians arrived, strong and ready to work hard for little money. In America, there were more jobs than they had ever seen in Italy.

But everything about America was strange to the Italians. The traffic, the noise, the endless rows of apartments five and six stories high that blocked the sky—these sights and sounds made a big impression on the immigrants. Suddenly, they remembered the cramped, one-room house in the hillside town in Italy as full of sunlight and fresh air. They recalled their miserable lives in the Old Country with great affection and longing.

America seemed cold and unhelpful; Italy was bathed in the warm glow of fond memories. It was their home, the home of their hearts. They said that America only wanted the brains and muscles of Italians, it cared nothing for their feelings. The Italians were lonely for the trees and hills they knew so well in Italy, and they could not bring themselves to trust this new country and its people.

The immigrants were surrounded by the strange sounds of English. To their ears it was just noise and didn't make any sense. Newcomers had to rely on other immigrants to teach them English and to help them make their way through their first days. Imagine not knowing how to count the money, how to say hello, or how to ask for directions.

Library of Congress

A peddler selling Italian bread

Emma Pioli and her children went through Ellis Island and took the ferry to the train station. There, they boarded a train to Ladd, Illinois, where Papa worked in a mine. They had no money left and spoke no English. On the train a woman passed through their compartment several times selling fruit. She felt sorry for Roberto and gave him a banana. He had never seen a banana, but the woman indicated that it was good to eat. He bit into it. It was terrible! He sat, confused, with the banana in his lap. When the woman passed through again, she noticed with dismay that he hadn't peeled the fruit! She showed him how, and Roberto ate his first banana.

Italian immigrants gather around a pushcart, looking for deals

The immigrants first learned the English words they needed in their work, as well as other common words like bread, milk, and water. They also mixed English and Italian together into a language that only other Italian immigrants and the Americans who worked with them could understand. This "Italglish" was also useful to Italians who could not understand each other's regional dialects. In "Itaglish" the word "job," for example, became *giobba*, "picnic" was *picchnicca*, "work" was *vorche*, and "teacher" was *ticcia*. The famous baseball player Babe Ruth was called *Il Bambino* or *Bigga Bambino*. The Fourth of July was called *Il Forte Gelato*, which actually means "the Great Freeze," but the sound was similar. "Railroad" was called *re erode*, again because it sounded like the English word. *Re* means "king" in Italian, which gives you a sense of the role the railroad played in the lives of the men who worked on it.

Shoeshine boys ready to work

SETTLING IN THE CITIES

During the decades of heavy immigration, 1900 to 1920, New York had a larger population of Italians than Florence, Venice, and Genoa combined. In 1910 New York was home to 340,000 Italians, more than in any other American city.

Since most immigrants had never even visited a city, much less lived in one, it may seem odd that they chose to settle in such an unfamiliar environment. But the immigrants came with very little money, so many were forced to find work immediately right where they landed, which for most was New York City. Farming in America was very different from farming in Italy, and besides, they wanted a change of fortune. They did not cross 4,000 miles of ocean to go right back to the troubles of farming! In addition, many immigrants planned to stay just long enough to save money. The sensible thing to do was to settle in the cities where work was plentiful and easy to find.

Domenico Castelli was a boy when his family immigrated to New York City. His father worked ten hours a day digging ditches and laying pipe. When there was no work, he'd sit with his friends at the kitchen table and play cards. Domenico went to school and made friends with a group of Italian boys from his neighborhood. At school there were also Irish and German boys, and after school they would throw rocks at each other and steal sweet potatoes from the street vendors. They went down to the river to rummage through the dumps, looking for things to sell. When his father had a lot of work, he'd give Domenico pennies every now and then to buy candy. He loved candy—it was something he'd never had in Italy.

Candy was a big treat for immigrant kids

24

Mulberry Street was the center of a bustling Italian neighborhood in New York City

Most immigrants settled in a bustling, crowded neighborhood full of other Italian immigrants. This area of town became known as "Little Italy." Immigrants from the same Italian towns or provinces lived near one another in the same apartment building or on the same street. Even though Italians settled together in the same neighborhoods, it took some time before they lost their sense of local identity and began to feel that they were simply Italian, and not, for example, Calabrian or Sicilian. It took even longer before they began to feel that they were American.

In a world that was so unfamiliar, the immigrants found comfort in an environment where some things were familiar. The immigrants worked hard to recreate some of the sights, smells, and sounds of the Old World. They had their own bakeries and grocery stores and produce markets. They could buy Italian bread, cheeses, olive oil, and spices. Italians were successful at small farming, turning empty city lots into family vegetable gardens filled with Italian tomatoes, parsley, eggplant, and fava beans. They held festivals for the feast days of saints, just as they had in Italy.

One of the most important days in Italian East Harlem in New York City was July 16, the feast of the Madonna of Mt. Carmel. They celebrated with food stalls, fireworks, music, and a religious procession. Although a neighborhood might be called Little Italy, it was in fact never entirely Italian. The other immigrants—German, Jewish, Polish, and Irish—would often join in the festivities as well.

Purchasing block ice from a street merchant

PREJUDICE

Most Americans decided what Italians were like before they really knew anything about them. People thought every Italian was connected to crime and was always ready to kill for passion or revenge. Americans were also afraid that the newcomers were taking jobs from them. Italians were discriminated against because of their dark skin, customs, language, religion, and occupations. People called them cruel names and laughed at the way they dressed and talked.

The Italians meanwhile thought that Americans were heartless, with no concern for anything except making money. There was no emotion in American life, Italians said.

The Bettmann Archive

New Orleans residents storm the prison where 11 Italian Americans are held

Sam dreams that one day he will be the boss

Sam Passalacqua came to New York City by himself when he was just 13 years old. He rented a room in Italian East Harlem and got a job digging ditches. His boss yelled at him because he was Italian and didn't speak English. One day several men were struggling to lay sewage pipe. Sam knew how to do this. He excitedly tried to tell the boss that he could do a better job. The boss didn't understand him and pushed him roughly back to his place, calling him "a stupid dago kid." Sam vowed that one day he would have that man's job. He remembered his grandfather's saying, "He who acts like a sheep, the wolf will eat." He would not be a sheep, he would be the wolf, the boss. Each time he was treated badly simply because he was Italian, he was inspired to work harder and improve his life. Sam eventually became a successful businessman and ran several of his own companies.

Italians could get only the worst housing and the worst jobs. They were treated badly and often accused of crimes they didn't commit. In 1890, for example, seven Italians were arrested in New Orleans when the Chief of Police said, as he lay dying, that "dagos" killed him. When the Italians were found not guilty, the people of New Orleans didn't believe that they were innocent. Townspeople marched to the jail where the men were still being held, and they hung the men, including four other Italians who had no connection to the case at all.

In perhaps the most famous case of prejudice against Italians, two men were executed without a fair trial. Nicola Sacco and Bartolomeo Vanzetti were Italian immigrants who spoke little English. They were accused in the murder of two men in a robbery attempt in South Braintree, Massachusetts, in 1920. At the trial, the facts that they were Italian immigrants and anarchists (people who believe there should be no government) were considered reasons enough to find the two men guilty. Their lawyer appealed the case several times as evidence to prove their

Many Americans thought that all Italian immigrants were beggars

innocence was found. The appeals had no effect, and the men were executed in 1927. Before his death, Vanzetti said, "I'm going to die because I'm Italian, and I am Italian. I'm going to die because I'm an anarchist, and I am an anarchist." But neither being Italian, nor being an anarchist, is a crime. The case of Sacco and Vanzetti is still hotly debated today, but whether they were guilty or innocent will never be known. What is clear is that they could not get a fair trial in the 1920s.

Sacco (right) and Vanzetti

Italians often faced prejudice in the courts

27

LIVING AND WORKING CONDITIONS

The immigrants left behind a life poor in food, money, and work but rich in fresh air, peaceful living, and family happiness. Now they lived in overcrowded, ugly apartments in New York, Chicago, and Philadelphia. They endured constant noise and dirt, and the stifling feeling of hundreds of families living so close together. But there were unexpected luxuries, too, such as a toilet just down the hall and the convenience of running water.

The Italians had the worst choices of places to live, and they also took the worst jobs. If you were a stonemason, a shoemaker, a fisherman, or some other skilled laborer, perhaps you could find a job doing the same thing in America. But most Italian men became garbage collectors, street peddlers, or ditch diggers. Italians laid thousands of

Laborers wait in an employment line

Some of America's most successful labor leaders were Italians. They organized workers and fought for labor unions, better pay, and worker's rights. Arturo Giovannitti and Guiseppe Ettor led the famous 1912 strike in a Lawrence, Massachusetts, textile factory. It was a long strike, with more than 300 people arrested and one worker killed during a clash with police. All of the workers' children were sent out of town for safety. The strikers won, but they gained a raise of only one cent an hour. But their problems had been heard. It was revealed that young children worked in the factory, and that the workers were underfed and had to live in dark, unsafe huts. The strike succeeded in exposing the plight of the factory workers to the public.

A family works together at the kitchen table making artificial flowers

miles of railroad track across America, and they mined coal, copper, and tin. They helped build the subways, buildings, and roads. The American economy provided more opportunity and a greater variety of jobs than Italians had had in Italy.

In those days, there were no laws that guaranteed workers the same pay for the same work. In 1906 Italian ditch diggers were paid $1.46 for a ten-hour day while an Irishman might make $2.00. Even so, Italians saved their money carefully, often sending as much as two-thirds of their income back to Italy. For very little money, Italians worked hard and kept a cheerful attitude. And they took pride in their work. Their beautiful tile work can still be seen in the New York subways, and their graceful stonework appears on buildings throughout several American cities. Their artistic sense and skill added warmth and beauty to America.

Women worked as well. They rented out rooms in their houses and assembled cigars or artificial flowers at home. It was against Italian tradition for women to have jobs alongside men, so they worked only at home or in the garment factories with other women.

Until 1900 many Italians found work through a *padrone*, a labor agent who brought together workers and employers. Padrones helped men find work, took care of their banking, wrote letters for them, and provided room and board. But the padrones often charged high prices or cheated the men. As Italian immigrants became familiar with the American economy and learned to speak the language, they no longer needed the padrones.

FAMILY AND RELIGION

It was the children who changed Italian family life in America. Daughters had more freedom than they ever were allowed in Italy. They held jobs, made their own money, and went to school. Girls argued with their parents for the right to keep some of their wages for themselves and to go out to ice cream parlors with friends. Parents were uncomfortable with this new world, a world they lived in but did not fully understand. Fathers were not used to having to rely on their sons for help in reading forms or talking to officials. But the children knew more about life in America because they went to school, learned English, and quickly adapted to American ways.

At first, parents didn't understand the importance of school for their children because they still needed them to work to help pay rent and buy food. And they were outraged that recreation was provided at school. Children went to school to *play*? In addition, they thought the oatmeal the children were served in school for breakfast was fit for pigs, not people! But parents slowly changed, and eventually they encouraged their children to study hard.

Some Italians shortened their names or changed them entirely to blend more easily into American culture. DiFilippo became Phillips, Castaniogla became Castanola. But most Italians were not willing to abandon their family name so easily and they patiently spelled it out for others and pronounced it over and over again.

U. T. The Institute of Texan Cultures

Italian families gather in front of their church

The Catholic Church in America was run by the Irish, not by the Italians. Some families went to church, but when the basket was passed to collect money, Papa refused to put anything in it. He mumbled that he didn't have to pay to pray. The Irish frowned upon the Italian saint day celebrations, the good luck charms they wore, and their worship of the Madonna. So Italians went to church only occasionally and continued to observe their saint day celebrations, keep their home shrines, and say their own prayers. Gradually, as small local churches that suited Italian tastes were established, Italian families went to church more often.

Many Italians had large families in America, just as they had in the Old Country

Although everyone worked very hard, there was some time for leisure activities, which had been rare in Italy. Men played *bocci* ball (lawn bowling) and drank *cappucinos* in cafés. Women listened to opera and dressed in colorful clothing, not just the somber black dresses they had worn in the Old Country.

A skilled bocci *player*

Children played stickball in the streets, went to parks, and bought cream sodas with friends. Everyone wore shoes. On weekends fathers changed from their work clothes into ironed pants, a fresh white shirt, a tie, and shined shoes. Families moved into nicer neighborhoods, bought comfortable furniture, electric lights, and carpets. Christmas was a thrill as they dug their savings from Mason jars buried in the yard and bought games, clothing, nuts, and dried fruits to be shipped to their relatives in Italy.

Interestingly, they enjoyed Italian culture in America as they never had in Italy. Now, they listened to opera, went to Italian theater, and ate fine Italian food. Their diet expanded to include salamis, chicken, fish, and Italian desserts and cheeses. They could eat these things every evening, not just on special days once a month. They even ate other ethnic foods, such as Polish sausage, German beer, and Jewish pastries. Life was richer and more varied in every way.

MAKING PROGRESS IN AMERICA

Italians began to move all over the country. They worked in mines in Illinois and homesteaded in Wisconsin. They laid railroad track in Washington and farmed in Oregon and California. They became fishermen and importers in Louisiana and cowboys in Texas. Everywhere they went, Italians brought their craftsmanship and their drive to improve their lives.

Charlie Albert Siringo was one such Italian-American success story. He rode the range as a cowboy in Texas and later became a detective for the Pinkerton Agency. He was an expert with a gun, but he never killed anyone—he liked people too much. With his slender frame he fooled many into thinking he wasn't tough, but he was smart, quick, and courageous. He tracked Billy the Kid and Butch Cassidy's Wild Bunch. He wrote about his experiences as a cowboy detective, and the book was such a success it launched the popular genre of cowboy fiction.

There were many other success stories in the Italian-American community as Italian immigrants and their children became more established in American society. Most families got ahead through constant work and gradual progress. The father would first work for a few years on the railroads or digging canals, while the mother and daughters assembled cloth flowers at home and the boys delivered bread for the local bakery, collected scrap, or worked with their father. Next, the father might get a job in construction, where he could make a little more money, building subway stations and houses. With every member of the family working, they could save enough money to open a bakery or grocery store. Everyone helped out at the store and held some other job as well. Perhaps the girls worked in a cotton mill and the mother took

Rosa Mondavi was a remarkable Italian immigrant. She began her life in America in a Minnesota mining town, where she took in boarders to increase her family's income. For 14 years, she always had 15 men in her house, plus her husband and children. She was a mother to all: washing their clothes, cleaning the house, and demanding perfect behavior from everyone. She worked from five in the morning until near midnight— with none of the modern conveniences we take for granted, like a washing machine, dishwasher, or store-bought bread.

Rosa Mondavi served her boarders three home-cooked meals every day

Domenico Ghirardelli keeps his cheerful chocolate makers busy

in boarders. They saved more money and expanded their shop, opened a small factory, or bought land. Their method was always to work hard, save money, take risks, and employ the entire family.

Italian immigrants were not afraid to gamble and often bought an unknown piece of land no one else wanted, or they opened a business, trusting that they would be successful. Parents believed the best way to give their children a future was to start a family business, own a store or bakery, or farm a piece of land.

The Italians were especially successful in California. San Francisco had the richest Italian community in all the United States. There were bankers, merchants, fish brokers, farmers, vintners (people who make wine), and chocolate makers. Domenico Ghirardelli opened a candy store during the California Gold Rush. *His* gold was his discovery of the many uses of ground chocolate. Today, chil-

dren of employees from as far back as 1860 still work at the famous Ghirardelli Chocolate Factory near Fisherman's Wharf.

An Italian-American cobbler

SAN FRANCISCO'S NORTH BEACH

North Beach is not a beach at all. It's a neighborhood in San Francisco between two big hills, Telegraph Hill and Russian Hill. It has been an Italian neighborhood for a very long time.

Imagine taking a stroll through this lovely neighborhood. Columbus Avenue, named after Cristoforo Colombo, cuts at an angle from downtown to the wharf, slicing through the middle of North Beach. You can stand on Columbus Avenue and look one way down to the cold blue waters of the San Francisco Bay, or the other way to the high-rises downtown, with the Transamerica pyramid building pointing like a needle into the sky. You can admire the narrow white houses wedged side by side up Russian Hill in front

of you. They are tall, with carved woodwork around the doors and big windows that look out over the bay. Behind you is Telegraph Hill, with more narrow houses and Coit Tower, where you can watch the fog roll over the neighborhood in the evening.

As customers step out of the nearby Caffé Puccini, you can hear the sounds of opera coming from inside the café. The smell of garlic cooking is in the air, mixing with the exhaust fumes from the buses and cars moving up and down Columbus Avenue.

You enter the Stella Pastry and Café and consider what to eat. It's cool and quiet inside. Inside the glass case are sweets such as biscotti, cannoli, panettoni, and Sacrepantina. Sacrepantina is not the name of a food, it's an exclamation of delight and wonder—

All dressed up for a North Beach carnival

34

Italians are famous for their tasty baked goods

like saying "holy cow!" in English. It's a light, sweet spongecake layered with zabaglione cream, a special Italian cream that has to be hand-whipped in a copper bowl to achieve a perfect taste and texture. Sacrepantina is a "holy cow!" kind of dessert. Try a piece.

After dessert you walk into the old Italian church on Washington Square Park. It smells of candle wax. The stained glass windows filter beautifully colored bits of sunlight into the dim air. Back on the street you hear three languages spoken: English, Italian, and Chinese. San Francisco's Chinatown is beside North Beach and the two neighborhoods blend together. You pass Italian restaurants, more bakeries, and more cafés. The windows of Molinari's delicatessen are filled with wheels of cheeses, boxes of pastas, special cookies from Italy, and salamis hanging from hooks in the ceiling. Molinari's has been in North Beach since 1896. The Working Man's clothing store around the corner has been supplying North Beach with sturdy work pants and shirts for eighty years.

San Francisco's Italian community has lived in North Beach since the days of California's Gold Rush, which began in 1848. Italians have been here so long the neighborhood feels like a family. The man who owns Molinari's knows the man who owns the Caffé Puccini who knows the man who owns the Stella Café, and so on. Their forebears are all from different parts of Italy and they all still speak Italian. They think of Italy with affection, but life in America has been good to them and San Francisco is their home.

A feast in celebration of St. Joseph

GERALDINE FERRARO

When the going gets tough, what do you do? Do you want to stop and do something else? When you lose do you feel like a loser? Former Congresswoman Geraldine Ferraro showed us how to get through difficulties with grace and dignity, and not fold when the pressure is on. And she showed us that winning is more than the final score. Winning is being yourself, doing the best job possible, giving your all, and telling the truth. She came out a winner, even though she and Walter Mondale lost the 1984 presidential election.

Geraldine Ferraro made history when she became the first woman vice presidential nominee for the Democratic Party in 1984. She had many loyal supporters during the campaign. But she also received criticism from the press and from her opponents. Ferraro learned what it was like to be at the center of a storm of public attention, not all of it friendly.

Born in 1935 in Newburgh, New York, Geraldine Ferraro had a childhood similar to many people's. Her parents were Italian immigrants. Her father died when she was only eight, and her mother worked hard to provide for her family. Geraldine knew that education was her best ticket to success. She became a teacher and taught second grade while she went to law school at night. As a lawyer she became Assistant District Attorney in Queens, New York, where she headed a special section for victims of violent crime. This was a difficult job. She wanted to have more of an effect on the choices people have in life. So she ran for Congress from her district in New York, and she won. As a United States Represen-

The Bettmann Archive

Ferraro was the first woman to become a vice presidential nominee

Ferraro's last name comes from the Italian word *ferro*, which means "iron"—something that can be bent but not broken. It is a fitting name for a person who never gives up, no matter what obstacles she meets. Ferraro says that her father's death when she was eight years old changed her life forever. She discovered at an early age how easily things can be taken away, and she learned to focus on what's really important. Perhaps Geraldine learned to persist from her mother. After Geraldine's father died, she took up bead work and went without meat so she could send her two children to good schools.

The Democratic vice presidential candidate addresses supporters on the campaign trail

tative she was known for her hard work and her skill in bringing people together.

All this time, she was married and a mother to three children. Can you imagine your mom as a Congresswoman and a vice presidential candidate? For Ferraro, as for so many Italian Americans, her family was at the center of her life. She loved her children and her husband, and they cheered her on.

Imagine her dismay when, as the vice presidential nominee, her family was attacked in the press. Her family's financial dealings were questioned and her husband was accused of having connections to the Mafia (Italian American organized crime). Unfortuately, many Americans still believed that powerful Italian Americans must be part of the Mafia. Ferrarro countered these accusations by telling the simple truth with grace and a sense of humor.

A presidential campaign is like running a marathon, month after month. Candidates endure long days of preparing policy, giving speeches, and traveling around the country meeting people. Everywhere Ferraro went, people came out to see and hear the first female vice presidential candidate. Ferraro is known for her speaking ability, her dedication to solving problems, and her skill in talking to people on a personal level. She continues to lead an active life of public service.

Ferraro answers reporters' questions

FAMOUS ITALIANS IN AMERICA

Mother Cabrini (1850–1917)

Sister Francesca Cabrini arrived in New York after a long trip from Italy on the last windy day of March in 1889. She was accompanied by five other sisters of her order. They found a room to spend the night in, with insects climbing the walls and mice running across the floor. This was not a shining beginning in the New World. There was no convent waiting for her and nobody to welcome her, but she was not dismayed. Mother Cabrini, as she soon was called, had a talent for making things happen. First, she found a basement to rent and opened a school to teach girls embroidery. Then she started a day nursery to help poor children keep off the streets. Next, she opened a hospital. She eventually left the Missionary Sisters of the Sacred Heart to set up more hospitals, orphanages, and schools. She was a smart businesswoman with a special flair for buying worthless property that would one day be very valuable. She walked through cities, tirelessly searching for a run-down building she could buy and transform. Until the day she died she worked to make other people's lives better, and in 1946 she was made a saint, becoming America's first. Her feast day is November 13.

Governors Mario Cuomo (b. 1932) and Ella Grasso (1919–1981)

Mario Cuomo grew up in a poor neighborhood in Queens, New York, and he didn't speak English until he began school. His parents were poor, hardworking immigrants who never dreamt their son would grow up to be one of New York's most popular governors. Cuomo learned from his parents about working hard and giving one's best, and about the importance of family. He is famous for his inspiring speeches and for his liberal politics.

Ella Grasso was another groundbreaking Italian American in politics. She was Connecticut's, and the country's, first woman governor. Like Cuomo, her parents were hardworking immigrants; her mother worked in a cotton mill, and her father owned a bakery. She grew up aware that people disliked her family because they were Italian, and for no other reason. She never forgot her beginnings when she became Governor of Connecticut.

Mother Cabrini, America's first saint

The notorious gangster Al Capone

Al Capone (1899–1947)

The gangsters of the 1920s were Irish, Jewish, and Italian. Prohibition (1919 to 1933), when alcohol was illegal, produced some of our flashiest gangsters. Al Capone was one of them. Born in Brooklyn in 1899, Capone ruled the Chicago underworld of crime and bootlegging liquor with a flair and style that was hard to match. Prohibition was an unpopular law, and Capone inspired admiration among some for defying it. He was an excellent businessman, wore specially tailored suits, had a large library, and ate the finest foods. He believed he was doing the public a service by providing them with good whiskey and places to play cards. At the same time, he had a reputation for being a heartless killer. He was finally sent to prison for tax evasion and died in 1947.

Francis Ford Coppola (b. 1939)

So, you want to make movies? So did Francis Ford Coppola. When he was a child, he got polio and spent a year at home, paralyzed and with little to do but watch television. That was the beginning of his interest in movies. His parents were immigrants, and he was taught that Italians had a great culture. He grew up in the warmth of an extended Italian American family full of love and aunts and uncles. Coppola's goal has been to make experimental, imaginative movies. Like many Italians, he has employed members of his family in his work. Many of his films are classics. They include *Patton*, *The Godfather*, *Bram Stoker's Dracula*, and *Apocalypse Now*. He won four Academy Awards for one of his films about Italian American families, *The Godfather II*.

Born Madonna Louise Veronica Ciccone, this superstar is perhaps the most famous Italian American in the world. Madonna is known for her bold, often controversial, performing style.

CONTRIBUTIONS TO U.S. CULTURE

How many times have you eaten Italian food? Spaghetti and pizza, lasagne, salami, ravioli, mozzarella and parmesan cheese—they're all Italian. What are your favorite vegetables? How about artichokes, zucchini, and broccoli? Perhaps your parents occasionally drink a glass of California wine. All of these foods were brought to America by Italians. Italians have contributed much to American tastes in cooking and eating. There are thousands of Italian restaurants in the United States, and American families of all ethnic backgrounds make pasta dinners.

Not only have Italians given us a taste for a wide variety of foods, they have also contributed to their production. Italians have grown and marketed everything from top-notch red wine to orange juice, from artichokes and zucchini to peanuts. Tropicana, Chef Boyardee, Planters Peanuts, Gallo, and S & W Foods are just a few of the American companies that were launched by Italian immigrants.

The Bettmann Archive

Joe Montana is famous for his flawless passes

He's called "Golden Joe" and "Big Sky" for his magnificent passes. He holds several NFL passing records and has been honored as the Super Bowl's Most Valuable Player. Joe Montana (b. 1956) is possibly the best quarterback in NFL history. He became the best because he loves the game and works hard, improving his skill and performance through practice. He has taken the San Francisco 49ers to four Super Bowl championships.

Fiorello LaGuardia confers with First Lady Eleanor Roosevelt

Did you know that the Bank of America got its start as the Bank of Italy? A. P. Giannini originated the idea of branch and national banking, turning his small San Francisco Bank of Italy into the largest bank in America.

Do you listen to the music of Frank Sinatra, Frank Zappa, Madonna, or to Puccini operas? Italians brought their talent and love of music with them and there have always been popular Italian American musicians. Perhaps someone in your family was a fan of Yogi Berra or Rocky Marciano, just two Italian American sports heros. Maybe your grandparents remember Fiorello LaGuardia, one of New York's most beloved mayors, reading the Sunday comics to children over the radio when there was a big newspaper strike in New York.

Italians brought their talents as well as their attitudes and values with them to America. They believed that work was important and that quality was better than quantity. They brought beauty and art into every aspect of their lives, from the apartment window boxes planted with herbs and geraniums to the murals painted on the walls of restaurants, to the paintings of Frank Stella or the sculpture of Simon Rodia. Italians say that the heart comes before money, that it's better to be happy than rich. Finally, Italians brought with them a strong sense of family.

Italian cuisine is a favorite in America

ITALIAN AMERICANS TODAY

For the parents of an Italian immigrant family—the first generation—America was always a foreign place. They spoke Italian better than English, and they liked only Italian food and wanted only Italian friends. It was a big step when they stopped calling themselves Piolis from the province of Emilia-Romagna and became simply Italian. After that they slowly began to feel like Italian Americans.

For the children, or second generation, life was confusing. They spoke English on the streets, in school, and at work, but they spoke Italian at home. They lived right on the fence between old and new, always going back and forth. They loved their parents but

Italian-American hero Joe DiMaggio

The Bettmann Archive

Joe DiMaggio was the New York Yankees' greatest hitter. He was married to Marilyn Monroe, one of America's most beautiful movie stars. And he was the son of Italian immigrants. He was the first Italian-American hero, and he changed the way America thought about Italians. His father left the small island off the coast of Sicily, where the DiMaggios had always been fishermen, and came to America in the 1880s. They lived in a small house in an Italian neighborhood on Taylor Street in San Francisco. Eventually, his father bought his own fishing boat. Joe played for the San Francisco Seals and then the New York Yankees. He was a superb centerfielder and he still holds "the record that may never be broken" of getting hits in 56 consecutive games. Both of his brothers, Dom and Vince, played baseball as well. People said Joe was the best hitter, Dom the best fielder, and Vince the best singer.

U.T. The Institute of Texan Cultures

Many Italian Americans served in World War II

were embarrassed by their halting English and heavy accent, and by the old-fashioned way they dressed and lived. The children had both American and Italian friends, habits, and values.

WWII was a turning point for Italians in America. At the beginning they admired Benito Mussolini, the dictator of Italy, and felt proud to be Italian as their homeland became a world power. But the more they heard of Mussolini's repressive government, the less pride they felt. When the United States joined the war against Germany and its ally, Italy, there was no question for most Italian Americans that they were on America's side. Italian Americans feared, however, that they would be treated badly by the United States government or by American citizens. There were many tense months before the government announced that Italians living in America were not "enemy aliens." This was a loud and clear statement that American troops were fighting Mussolini and the Fascists he led, not the Italian people.

Even so, for Italian American families,

World War II was a fearful time. Many Italian Americans had beloved relatives in Italy, especially in the South. When American troops and their allies invaded Italy to stop Mussolini, Italian Americans worried about the safety of their Italian relatives—and about their own sons. Many soldiers in the American Army, Navy, and Air Force were sons of Italian immigrants. They fought proudly in the campaign against Italy, eager to serve their America and to help the people in the country they had come from.

Italian Americans have entered all professions

43

Italian Americans still spend much of their time with their families

American soldiers were able to communicate with the villagers. They shared their food with the villagers and, in turn, the villagers let the soldiers warm themselves by the hearth or sleep in their chicken huts. The soldiers sympathized with the Italians' tales of hardship. Life in Southern Italy had changed little since large numbers of immigrants had left decades earlier. People still lacked education and jobs, and many men still labored 15 hours each day in the fields. The buildings and homes in the villages were old and crumbling.

The war made living conditions even worse. Few Italians supported the aims of the dictator Mussolini. People wanted change, democracy, and opportunity, just as their parents and grandparents had. The Italian-American soldiers came to understand why their forebears had left Italy and, though they wanted to help the Italians, they felt proud to be Americans. Their service in the war earned them the respect of other Americans, and they began to feel more accepted as true Americans.

In the years following the war, many Italian Americans at last had enough money to send their children to college, expand their businesses, and even hire people from outside the family. The children became lawyers, doctors, and scientists. They moved out of the cities and into the suburbs.

Italians still spent much of their social time with their families. They lived near each other, often ate dinners together, and took care of each other's children. Today, Italian Americans may not speak Italian, but they are probably proud of their Italian roots. They play American sports like baseball and football, not bocci ball. Many date and marry people who are not Italian or even Catholic, although many still belong to the Catholic Church and send their children to Catholic schools. Italians have blended successfully into American life, keeping elements of their old traditions alive.

Other books about Italian Americans and immigration:

Brown, Wesley and Amy Ling, eds. *Visions of America: Personal Narratives from the Promised Land.* New York: Persea Books. 1993.

Krustrup, Erik V. *Gateway to America: New York City.* Creative Education Inc., 1982.

Mangione, Jerre. *America is also Italian.* New York: Putnam, 1969.

Santoli, Al. *New Americans, An Oral History: Immigrants and Refugees in the United States Today.* New York: Viking, 1988.

BIZARRE & BEAUTIFUL SERIES

A spirited and fun investigation of the mysteries of the five
senses in the animal kingdom.

Each title is 8¹/₂" x 11", 48 pages, $14.95 hardcover, with color
photographs and illustrations throughout.

Bizarre & Beautiful Ears
Bizarre & Beautiful Eyes
Bizarre & Beautiful Feelers
Bizarre & Beautiful Noses
Bizarre & Beautiful Tongues

RAINBOW WARRIOR ARTISTS SERIES

W hat is a Rainbow Warrior Artist? It is a person who
strives to live in harmony with the Earth and all living
creatures, and who tries to better the world while living
his or her life in a creative way.

Each title is written by Reavis Moore with a foreword by LeVar
Burton, and is 8¹/₂" x 11", 48 pages, $14.95 hardcover, with
color photographs and illustrations.

Native Artists of Africa (available 1/94)
Native Artists of North America

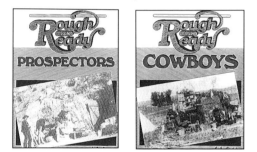

ROUGH AND READY SERIES

L earn about the men and women who settled the American
frontier. Explore the myths and legends about these courageous individuals and learn about the environmental,
cultural, and economic legacies they left to us.

Each title is written by A. S. Gintzler and is 48 pages, 8¹/₂" x 11",
$12.95 hardcover, with two-color illustrations and duotone
archival photographs.

Rough and Ready Cowboys (available 4/94)
Rough and Ready Homesteaders (available 4/94)
Rough and Ready Prospectors (available 4/94)

AMERICAN ORIGINS SERIES

M any of us are the third and fourth generation of our
families to live in America. Learn what our great-great
grandparents experienced when they arrived here and
how much of our lives are still intertwined with theirs.

Each title is 48 pages, 8¹/₂" x 11", $12.95 hardcover, with
two-color illustrations and duotone archival photographs.

Tracing Our German Roots, Leda Silver
Tracing Our Irish Roots, Sharon Moscinski
Tracing Our Italian Roots, Kathleen Lee
Tracing Our Jewish Roots, Miriam Sagan

ORDERING INFORMATION
Please check your local bookstore for our books, or call 1-800-888-7504 to order direct from us. All orders are shipped via UPS; see chart to calculate your shipping charge for U.S. destinations.
No P.O. Boxes please; we must have a street address to ensure delivery. If the book you request is not available, we will hold your check until we can ship it. Foreign orders will be shipped sur-
face rate unless otherwise requested; please enclose $3.00 for the first item and $1.00 for each additional item.

METHODS OF PAYMENT
Check, money order, American Express, MasterCard, or Visa. We cannot be responsible for cash sent through the mail. For credit card orders, include your card number, expiration date, and
your signature, or call (800) 888-7504. American Express card orders can be shipped only to billing address of cardholder. Sorry, no C.O.D.'s. Residents of sunny New Mexico, add 6.125% tax
to total.

Address all orders and inquiries to:
John Muir Publications
P.O. Box 613
Santa Fe, NM 87504
(505) 982-4078
(800) 888-7504

For U.S. Orders Totaling	Add
Up to $15.00	$4.25
$15.01 to $45.00	$5.25
$45.01 to $75.00	$6.25
$75.01 or more	$7.25

EXTREMELY WEIRD SERIES

All of the titles are written by Sarah Lovett, 8½" x 11", 48 pages, $9.95 paperbacks, with color photographs and illustrations.

Extremely Weird Bats
Extremely Weird Birds
Extremely Weird Endangered Species
Extremely Weird Fishes
Extremely Weird Frogs
Extremely Weird Insects
Extremely Weird Mammals
Extremely Weird Micro Monsters
Extremely Weird Primates
Extremely Weird Reptiles
Extremely Weird Sea Creatures
Extremely Weird Snakes
Extremely Weird Spiders

X-RAY VISION SERIES

Each title in the series is 8½" x 11", 48 pages, $9.95 paperback, with color photographs and illustrations and written by Ron Schultz.

Looking Inside the Brain
Looking Inside Cartoon Animation
Looking Inside Caves and Caverns
Looking Inside Sports Aerodynamics
Looking Inside Sunken Treasure
Looking Inside Telescopes and the Night Sky

THE KIDDING AROUND TRAVEL GUIDES

All of the titles listed below are 64 pages and $9.95 paperbacks, except for Kidding Around the National Parks and Kidding Around Spain, which are 108 pages and $12.95 paperbacks.

Kidding Around Atlanta
Kidding Around Boston, 2nd ed.
Kidding Around Chicago, 2nd ed.
Kidding Around the Hawaiian Islands
Kidding Around London
Kidding Around Los Angeles
Kidding Around the National Parks of the Southwest
Kidding Around New York City, 2nd ed.
Kidding Around Paris
Kidding Around Philadelphia
Kidding Around San Diego
Kidding Around San Francisco
Kidding Around Santa Fe
Kidding Around Seattle
Kidding Around Spain
Kidding Around Washington, D.C., 2nd ed.

MASTERS OF MOTION SERIES

Each title in the series is 10¼" x 9", 48 pages, $9.95 paperback, with color photographs and illustrations.

How to Drive an Indy Race Car
  David Rubel
How to Fly a 747
  Tim Paulson
How to Fly the Space Shuttle
  Russell Shorto

THE KIDS EXPLORE SERIES

Each title is written by kids for kids by the Westridge Young Writers Workshop, 7" x 9", with photographs and illustrations by the kids.

Kids Explore America's Hispanic Heritage
112 pages, $7.95 paper
Kids Explore America's African-American Heritage
128 pages, $8.95 paper
Kids Explore the Gifts of Children with Special Needs
112 pages, $8.95 paper (available 2/94)
Kids Explore America's Japanese Heritage
112 pages, $8.95 paper (available 4/94)

ENVIRONMENTAL TITLES

Habitats: Where the Wild Things Live
Randi Hacker and Jackie Kaufman
8½" x 11", 48 pages, color illustrations, $9.95 paper

The Indian Way: Learning to Communicate with Mother Earth
Gary McLain
7" x 9", 114 pages, illustrations, $9.95 paper

Rads, Ergs, and Cheeseburgers: The Kids' Guide to Energy and the Environment
Bill Yanda
7" x 9", 108 pages, two-color illustrations, $13.95 paper

The Kids' Environment Book: What's Awry and Why
Anne Pedersen
7" x 9", 192 pages, two-color illustrations, $13.95 paper